MW00939583

With Love

Stephaine Crosley

For more information: www.StephCrosley.com

Cover Design by Alexis Eckles Editing and Foreword by Meloni Williams

ISBN: 978-1536869453 First Edition: September 2016

10 9 8 7 6 5 4 3 2 1

Acknowledgements

First and foremost, I have to give all praises to the Man above. Every time I pray, I pray for guidance, reassurance, and I pray for Him not to give up on me, despite my inability to get it right the first several times. I pray for love. A love that is so pure and true. Of course, I have to give credit to my mother, Lou Crosley and father, Jerome Mann. My beautiful sisters: Bridgette, Nina and Jasmine who have been my biggest supporters. My handsome brother, Daniel Buie, whose creativity, talent and knowledge motivates me to be better. My beautiful nieces: Ja'Nya and Nitayvia, my handsome nephews: Jayvion, Khaumaurie and Aden, my beautiful God-daughters, Savannah and Bella...you all give me strength. Knowing that I create the belief in you that you can be anything you want to be makes me want to be everything I need to be. My Best friends, Glenna, Latoya, JaNay, Asia and Amanda thank you all for seeing my flaws and loving me despite them. My very close friends: Jona, Bridgette A., Que, Caroline, Janelle, Ackeeva, Montia, Tiara, Jasmine C. and my mentors: Gerry Howze and Melissa Muhammed thank you all for believing in me and pushing me to be my best self. To Tia and Leneal, thank-you for the experiences and lessons. To Shenita, Shawnita and Tristan, thank you for the time invested. To all of my friends and family, near and far, your presence in my life has contributed in some way to my growth as I hope I have and will continue to contribute to yours.

To everyone who believes in me, your support is inspiration. Together we stand. Together we are more powerful, but it starts with the love for self.

To Milwaukee, I love you.

Remember, in everything you do, do it with love.

Love. It is probably one of the smallest yet most powerful words. So many spend their lives in pursuit of its mystery. Some think it's an action, a verb—while others think it's something to be possessed or treasured and kept under lock and key. It is a word with definitions galore and expressions that constantly vary. Love isalso a word that teaches countless of lessons and often comes with baggage that, even as adults, we must learn to unpack or somehow figure out a way to hold along with everything else we struggle to carry.

Though love does not come one size fits all, it is important that we all experience it at least once along life's journey. From a mother or father's love, to self-love, to the romantic love that can be felt between two souls' bodies, whether ongoing or a memory, nobody is undeserving. With that understood, this book is a testament to prove that even you are worthy.

Stephaine's honesty and transparency serves as true encouragement that no matter your love experience—negative or positive—it is never too late to take control of it.

With Love provides readers the lens to not only examine your own love journey, but it also provides understanding and direction for you to be able to take responsibility for where you are on it. It takes the blame out of feeling loveless and the shame out of feeling unlovable, while confirming and reassuring that no matter what happened before or with anyone else, love is still able.

With Love provides the path to reflect and renew—to examine your truths and to get in touch with you. It is a quick and easy read, yet it is also unforgettable, and the value of its exercises is immeasurable. Stephaine is truly a woman of purpose who consistently practices what she preaches in her self-love sermons, so it's safe to say that there is something for everybody—man or woman—just beyond this page.

So, whether your heart is empty, partially or completely full, be sure to read with an open mind because it was written *with love* and possesses a message that is truly one of a kind!

"In order to reciprocate love,
you gotta notice it;
Gotta recognize it; gotta feel it first;
Gotta be let inside it—feel its hurt, and then
kneel to its worst.
If you contain it, don't hide it,
gotta reveal it first…
and when you think you hit rock bottom,
gotta feel it worse."
-Joe Budden

The night you were conceived, was it love? Are you a product of a one night stand, a love gone wrong, or were you part of a plan? When you were inside of your mother's womb, do you remember her singing or reading to you? Did you feel her hand as she rubbed her stomach at the thought of you being inside of her? Were you fed well—nice healthy foods to promote your growth inside of the womb? Or, do you remember the sour taste of alcohol or smoke filling your small lungs making it hard for you to mature comfortably? Do you remember the energy you felt while inside the womb—the energy of your mother? Her hurt, her joy, her disappointment, her sadness, her peace, her happiness? Do you remember when you first saw the light?

The day that you were born, was it love? When you took your first step, said your first word or used the potty for the first time…was it love? When you graduated from K-5, received your first "Superstar" award, participated in your first school musical, brought home your first piece of artwork, received your first shots, went to your first doctor's appointment, went on your first school field trip, or said your cutest saying, was it love?

Do you remember being hugged and told you're beautiful or being tucked in at night and read a bedtime story? Do you remember your parents being involved in school activities or at your sporting events, cheering you on? Do you remember both your mother and your father? Do you remember when your mother or father wiped your tears and told you, "It's going to be okay?"

Was it love?

For so long, I've struggled with understanding what love is. To this day, I still struggle. I have learned that love is a feeling, and how we have learned to embrace it depends greatly on how love was taught and given to us as children. Think about it when we are born, we are born into a world to two individuals whose responsibility is to love and care for us. Other than a higher power, our mother and father are the only two people we initially depend on for affection, love and attention. Anyone outside of our parents has the choice to love us or not. What if our parents make the choice not to love us and take care of their responsibility? From the very beginning our perception of love is tainted, and as we continue with life we struggle with really understanding love's true meaning and purpose. I struggle with connecting my childhood experiences to my idea of love and not understanding whether the experiences I remember were done out of responsibility or if they were done in love. As I think of love, all of the questions above and where I am currently in life, I've come to realize I do not think I fully know what love is. Though I have an idea, and I do know what love is not.

Love is not conditional;
love is not dependent on another variable.
Love is not tangible.
I don't think you can physically see love,
but you can feel it
by genuine and expressive actions.
Love is a feeling. Love is felt.
Growing up as a child, I did not feel it.
My foundation was tainted.
Was it really love?
Not that I can remember.

What is love?

[4]*"Love is patient, love is kind. It does not envy, it does not boast, it is not proud.* [5]*It does not dishonor others, it is not self-seeking, it is not easily angered, it keeps no record of wrongs.* [6]*Love does not delight in evil but rejoices with the truth.* [7]*It always protects, always trusts, always hopes, always perseveres."*

1 Corinthians 13:4-7

Was it with love? Do you remember?

Brainstorm:

Take a moment and create a list of your own childhood experiences through adolescence. In one column, list everything you perceived as good that has ever happened to you. In the second column, list everything you perceived as bad. As you continue reading the following section, keep that list in front of you.

Good Experiences Childhood through Adolescence	Bad Experiences Childhood through Adolescence

The Unconscious Mind

"But when something gives you nightmares,
can you afford to recollect it?"
– Joe Budden

As time goes by, we become older. Whether we become more mature or immature, however, depends on our upbringing, our environment, the people we surround ourselves with, our experiences and key relationships in our lives.

Take a minute to think about your childhood and where you are now. How much have you matured, and in what ways have you matured? What about from your teenage years to now? What about your early adulthood to now? Maturity is not an easy task, especially when there are no set guidelines for us to follow in order to achieve it—or to be able to recognize our achievement if/when we do reach it. Many of us are immature in nature for a number of different reasons—one being because we are not walking in our own truths. Immaturity is not always as blatant as most would think, but immaturity can prevent us from fostering meaningful relationships, communicating effectively and loving ourselves wholeheartedly. How we were brought up as children has a great impact on the current state of our maturity level, and most of us are not fully aware of it.

Sigmund Freud, neurologist, psychologist and physiologist in the 20th century, explored the structure of the mind and introduced three different levels of the mind: the conscious, the pre-conscious and the unconscious. The conscious mind consists of the thoughts we are aware of and focus on. Are you currently breathing? What are you focusing your eyes on? What is going on around you? These are all examples of our conscious mind. **What are you thinking about right now?** Our conscious mind keeps us in the present. The preconscious mind consists of the things that can be easily retrieved from our memory. The things in our preconscious are things we do not always think about but once asked, they are easy to remember—things such as our telephone number, address or birthday. **Recall the happiest day of your life so far.** Although, you were not currently thinking about it, when prompted, it was easy to remember. Lastly, there is the unconscious mind. Within our unconscious mind are the experiences we wish to forget about because they may be too hurtful and too frightening to relive, yet they have the most impact on our behavior. The unconscious mind is the most important piece in determining why we do the things we do and why we are able to do things with or without love. Although what is in our unconscious mind plays an integral role in why we do the things we do; often times we are not aware of this. We store past experiences in our unconscious mind. Past experiences are most responsible for our motives, decision-making abilities and feelings. **Think of one situation that you never want to re-live.** The experiences we push into our unconscious mind can gradually move from our unconscious to our preconscious to the forefront of our thoughts and feelings if we invested more time getting to know and understanding self.

Take a look at the list you created at the beginning of this section. How easy was it for you to retrieve the memories for the list of your good experiences? How easy was it for you to retrieve the list of your bad experiences? Now, think about where your conscious mind tends to slip to; does it see more positive than negative or more negative than positive? When you find yourself talking among a group of your peers, what theme represents the majority of your conversations? Is it happiness, positivity, bitterness, hurt, anger, uncertainty? What space in your life are you speaking from—is it from the surface or is it from a place deep inside? For instance, someone who has found themselves in one failed relationship after another, may always bring up the negative aspects of relationships, subconsciously, because they are speaking from a space of hurt. Although relationships have the potential to fail, a relationship is not a bad thing. When we never deal with the root of the problem though, of why the relationships we have been in failed, we begin adding baggage to our relationship by pushing the existing baggage to the back of our mind. Once another relationship fails, as human beings, we naturally hurt, and we speak from that emotional space as opposed to a more logical space. Our unconscious mind has so more control over us than we give it credit for. There is a reason someone is always speaking negative of someone else, why someone can always be so uplifting and positive, or why a person can never be alone.

Bringing memories from our unconscious mind is not an easy task; for that reason, it is important for us as humans to reflect in order to grow. What are you running from? What was too painful or frightening for you that you pushed it well past your memory in hopes you'd never have to experience it again? How does it impact your relationships today? The idea is not to relive troubled times but to understand them; understanding them will help you better understand you.

I reflect on myself often because I did not like the person I was. I was not a bad person, but I was not the person I wanted to be. So I had to ask myself, "What is holding you back?" For so long I tried to always be the person to shower others with love because I believe in being the energy you wish to receive; however, every time I tried to love, I pushed people away or stopped them from getting too close. How could this be? I did not like thinking back to the times I felt unwanted; it was hard to relive, so I thought by loving others I could fill that void.

I failed at it because I did not really know what or how to love and because of that, my love had conditions. I was running from abandonment. I figured, if you loved someone enough, they would not leave you, and I was tired of being left. I was running from love. I did not want anyone to love me out of fear that 1. They would abandon me, as a child I encountered so many inconsistencies; people coming in, people going out. 2. I was unlovable. Maybe I simply did not deserve love. Most of my encounters with people I thought "loved" me were not always ideal. 3. They would uncover my truths and I was afraid to be vulnerable. When you are vulnerable you appear to be weak and at this point of my life I could not afford to get weaker so I covered it up. All these things I was taught through experiences as a young child.

Everything we go through in life teaches us something. The only way we do not learn is if we choose not to. All of the heartbreaks, all of the disappointments, all of the failures, all of the times someone else was chosen over us...those were all lessons in disguise. Often times we are not aware of the lessons because we allow the pain of the experience to consume and cripple us, blurring our better judgement. We want to blame everything and everyone, instead of just dealing with the situation at hand. We then shift those experiences to our unconscious mind, pretending it is no longer there, while trying to move on. Nonetheless, it happened, and because it happened, it affects us. Throughout our lives, we all struggle, we all hurt, we all cry, we all experience life because no one is perfect and until we realize that, we will continue to move within the same cycle becoming comfortable and settling for mediocrity, or less than. However, with awareness of who we are and awareness of the experiences stored in our unconscious mind, we can all persevere. Just do it, *with love*.

Childhood matters.

There are a lot of things that transpire in our early years of life, which we vividly remember with all of the emotions and feelings attached to them. Then, there are the things we have repressed within our unconscious minds, to prevent living through them and the emotions and feelings repeatedly associated with them. Although we do not remember every encounter from conception to birth to our toddler years, so many of those experiences have had such a huge impact on our perceptions, thought processes and behaviors. Thinking back to your childhood and knowing where you are today—mentally and emotionally—was it love?

Look back at the list you created in the beginning of this section. Did those experiences come wrapped in love? If you have had the joy of becoming a parent, while reading this book, think about the interactions between you and your child. Is everything you're doing with your child being done with love? Change is indeed a part of life; however, who we become in the future is founded by who and what we were taught to be as children.

I personally cannot say that I remember much of my childhood…or maybe I've tried my best to push as much of it into my unconscious mind. After all, if you do not think about it, it does not exist...right? WRONG!

No matter how much any of us try to run from experiences that may have hurt us, we are reminded of them by our resistance, behavior, lack of excitement or reactions to anything similar. It all becomes a pattern, whether it is fear or simply not understanding what we do not know—we run every single time. We run, and we make excuses. We blame everything we go through on everyone else without recognizing and owning our own truths. Owning our own truths can hurt because no one wants to see themselves as less than good enough, but it is when we confront our truths that we allow ourselves to be free.

*"Momma said she loves me,
said she cares."*
–Joe Budden

I remember growing up without a father and with a mother who tried. I remember hearing my father was incarcerated for drugs before I was born, and I also remember those same drugs taking over my childhood when they took over my mother. I remember being put out of a house with my mother because of her drug habit and not having anywhere to go. I remember sleeping at a homeless shelter with my mother and sisters, being ridiculed at school when the secretary would announce, "Shelter kids, your bus is here," and not wanting to go to the bus so that the other kids would not notice she was talking about us. I remember not having any food to eat and having to go with my mother to jump in one of the huge dumpsters outside of the local grocery store to gather the expired food they had thrown out. I remember being left at home for long hours with my sister with only our imaginations to create some sense of excitement. Even the time I broke my younger sister's leg and the ambulance had to come—my mom was nowhere in sight. "Why didn't the social workers come and take us away?" I remember thinking. I remember missing close to 100 days of school 4th grade year because we did not have adequate clothing or anyone to get us ready. I only remember that because I remember my teacher, Mrs. Thundercloud, pulling me to the side and asking me about it. "Why didn't the social workers come and take us away?" I thought again.

I always wondered if my life would have been better if the social workers did come and take me and my sister from my mother. However, after experiencing life's journey, it makes better sense that they did not. My mother could have completely abandoned us or left us on the curb to tend to her drug habit, but she didn't. Most people would probably think that does not make sense because she did not provide us with the ideal childhood and there were instances in which her drug habit was more important. We did struggle a lot as children because of her choices, but the way I look at it is: I am still here. She made sure we had a bed at the shelter and, although it was not the ideal meal, she still tried even if it meant digging in a trash can to get it. My mother developed a habit that she couldn't shake, yet she never forgot about us. That had to be love, right?

At least that was her definition, and my perception as a child of what love was: not having to choose between two things you love, while always trying to accommodate both - a lesson I learned early. As a young adult, when I came across two individuals who loved me, instead of choosing between the two I tried to accommodate both; because that was love as I knew it. Or was it selfish of me to have both, not considering the hurt and damage it causes as long as my needs are met? I did not know then, but I know now; my mother taught me that by the way she loved me.

I remember nights when my mother did not come home and other nights when we had to walk to the neighborhood "crack houses" to find her. I remember watching my mother being beaten by her brother once— my uncle—for stealing something of his to support her drug habit that he fed. Was that love? Condoning something until it no longer benefits us? Or was that selfish? Love isn't selfish.

"Said if I need her,
she'll always be there...
even her saying that struck me as weird."
— Joe Budden

I remember not having school clothes and not being able to go to school because of it. I remember my mother stealing all of my sister's money she made selling candy to fund a school trip. I remember feeling my mother's hands running over my body while I slept, trying to locate the dollar or two I hid in my panties so she wouldn't find it. I remember me and my little sister making baggies with tissue stuffed in them pretending we were selling drugs because this was our perception of life.

I do not recall my mother ever coming to school functions, and I cannot remember her being at any of my middle school basketball games. I do remember waking up on Christmas and not having gifts or the one time she wrapped up some of our old items so that it felt like Christmas. This taught me that love is making the best of your circumstances. Or was it that some circumstances can be avoided by making better decisions out of love?

I remember on birthdays when my mother would give gifts, steal them back and sell them to neighbors to support her habit. Was love doing whatever you had to do to feel that high, even if it means hurting people along the way? I remember not wanting anyone to see or know who my mother was. Was that love? Hiding what you are ashamed of because people would not approve of her, yet someone who secretly means so much to you?

A girl's first love is her father.

When things got really bad, I remember wanting my father to be there to save me. He never was. Is that what love consists of? Unrealistic thoughts?

I remember my father writing me from prison. I also remember in my earlier years when he sent gifts on Christmas from jail. That was cool at the time, but no amount of gifts could fill the void of emptiness I felt. I remember him being released right after I turned 14 years old and wanting absolutely nothing to do with him because, at that point, I had been through enough, and there I was preparing for my 8th grade graduation. Who needs a parent at that point? In my eyes, my mother tried, my dad did nothing.

In hindsight, although my father was locked up (based on a choice he made) I resented him for not being there to protect me, to love me, to take care of me. In my mind, although I did not have a relationship with him, I knew that my dad was responsible for me being here. I also witnessed the relationship my friends had with their fathers and knew that this was the only other person on earth, after my mother, that could save me and when he didn't I became numb toward him. I remember any time I would get into trouble or if I was going through a difficult patch, I would literally yell, "I can't wait until my dad gets out so I can move with him." However, it was like coming to the realization that what you knew to be true: Santa Clause, the Tooth Fairy, the Easter Bunny was all make believe; so I gave up in believing in a "father." I started to believe a father is just another made up character. Besides, neither of my sisters' fathers were around either, so maybe that was the way it was supposed to be. After being released, and a couple of attempts at building a relationship, he gave up on me. I was a stubborn child, but I was still a child who needed a father, and he was a father who was still a child. He simply did not know how to be a father.

*"Tell my Pop I ain't bothered when he don't
speak to me, I love you but it's weak to me.
On one hand, life is short and there's no
excuse to do it, but you was missing half my
life dog, I'm kind of used to it"*
– Joe Budden

Was this love? If something doesn't happen in the timeframe we want it to or the way we envision it happening, are we supposed to give up? I do not think so, and of course he was operating from his level of understanding and I from mine—the difference being I did not bring him into the world, but he helped bring me. What I have learned is that with patience comes compromise. Things do not always work on our time, and in order to get the results we want, we have to put in the work –even when it is not warm and fuzzy. What is love?

I remember missing my mother and what she used to be and not understanding how to be a daughter to a man I didn't know. With so many images of what a mother or father is supposed to be, not knowing or understanding your circumstances can lead you to a dark place, an unknown place. We are born into this world alone, and the only people obligated to love us are the two people responsible for creating us.

As people, we learn through experience. Our first encounter of love comes from our parents. Our parents set the tone and lay down the foundation, and that is regardless of whether they decide to be active parents or whether they decide to have nothing at all to do with us—leaving us for someone else to raise. So many of us are lost, so many of us do not know how to love, and even more of us do not know how to accept it because our foundation of love is tainted, or maybe it was never built. As a result, when we try to love someone else who has been tainted at some point in their life, we fail. Why?

Think about it: there is no true consistency to parenting styles. How you learned what love is, often times, is completely different from how the person you are interested in learned what love is. We all become fixated on operating in our own space. When that happens, we fail to give ourselves a chance because we believe what we know to be true, and they believe what they know to be true, so we bump heads and lack understanding, but we also lack guidance in knowing how to let our guards down, be vulnerable and compromise. Sometimes we have to steer away from what we know and be open to new because we're all tainted; we are all broken pieces. Loving and being loved requires teamwork, whether in a parent-child relationship, a friendship, or an intimate relationship. It all requires teamwork, and the mutual goal to love with the understanding that we have to meet each other where we are, which requires us to be honest in where we are.

Some of us watched our fathers beat our mothers, and then we watched our mothers stay. Some of us watched our mothers take care of our fathers, hand and foot. Some of us have siblings with different mothers, but have never seen our parents separated. Some of us watched our mothers and fathers work together to build an empire. Some of us watched our mother or father abandon us, leaving us to be raised by a single parent. Some of us watched our parents struggle, putting themselves last to make sure we had what we needed. Some of us watched our world crumble down behind closed doors, but to the outside world our home appeared perfect. Some of us watched both of our parents abandon us. Some of us watched the begging and pleading, the "I love you," the marriage, the tears, the divorce, the happiness, the togetherness, the aloneness. You tell me: Was it all done with love? What is love? How do you know?

When you feel alone in this big world of billions of people and you can't call on the only two people obligated to love you, how could you ever know what love is?

Love Lessons From My Parents

1. Love is selfish. You should never have to choose
2. Love is dependent on convenience. It is conditional
3. Give up on love if it is not working on your time
4. Love is inherited and does not require work
5. Love is never telling someone they are beautiful or showing affection

"Love is relative to whomever it stems from. If the seed is weak how could the love be strong? How could love not be prideful when that's all the giver of it knows?"
– Joe Budden

What lessons about love have you learned from your parents?

Reflect: Take a moment to think about the interactions you have had with your parents.

Make a list of the things you remember about both your mother and father.

Next to each item, list the emotion associated with that memory.

Experiences with Mother	Emotions associated with this experience

Experiences with Father	Emotions associated with this experience

Now: Think about the men and/or women in your life.

Are they anything like your father?
Or are you just like your father?
What about your mother?

Name of man/woman in your life	Favorite characteristic about him/her	Which parent does this person remind you of?	Why is this person in your life? (Reflect)

How is your relationship with your mother?

How is your relationship with your father?

Are you able to maintain relationships with other men/women? Why or why not?

Are there any memories from the above created lists that you can write others names to in addition to your mother or father? What, if any, are the similarities of those relationships that might have resulted in that?

Next: <u>Define love</u>.

What is it? How does it feel?

How do you show it, and in what ways do you accept it?

Are there certain obligations that must be met before you allow someone to love you?

Do those definitions, descriptions, and/or expectations differ between different "kinds" of relationships: romantic, friendship, family, etc.? If so, how?

As people, we are natural sponges. We soak in everything that happens around us. The beauty in being an adult is that we have the ability to decipher how much we soak in on the surface, and we can add that to what we already know.

As children, we do not have that option. As children we are taught by our surroundings, our environments and the actions of our caretakers, or lack thereof. What we observe around us is the "right" way to do things because in our young minds, we have nothing else to compare it to.

Your childhood is a time in which you are innocent and should live freely. However, what happens when that is taken away from you, and you have to grow up quickly? What happens when you have to figure out life by yourself? LIFE HAPPENS, AND YOU FIGURE IT OUT!

You do not give up; you do not stay stagnant. No matter how happy you are or how broken you may be, there is still someone waiting to absorb every emotion, every action and every word you say.

To the parents: What energy are you allowing your child to absorb from you?

Do you hope for them to walk in your footsteps, or do you encourage them to create their own?

What are you currently exposing your child(ren) to?

Is it assisting in their growth or are you boxing him/her in?

Activity for parents: Make a list of the negative energy that you might be allowing your children to absorb (You may not be fully aware of them, and most of them may exist in your unconscious mind—things such as the environment, the way you talk to them, if you tend to argue in front of them, what media you expose them to, etc.)

This is to help you consciously identify what you project onto your child(ren), so it can be brought to the conscious with hopes that when it happens, you are able to recognize and rectify it right then and there.

Similarly, create a list of the things you do intently with hopes that your child(ren) will absorb them, and what you do or can do to help bring those things out of them.

Negative Energy (actions, environment, company) your child absorbs	Positive Energy (actions, environment, company) your child absorbs

Yearning for that motherly love—
"Mama's baby, Papa's maybe."
-Unknown

Despite anything and everything, to this day, I still love my mother. It's that unconditional love between a mother and a child. I think women, mothers in particular, are some of God's greatest and strongest creations. My mother, as all mothers do, had an option to abort me, to give me up, to completely abandon me and—despite her drug addiction, she did none of those. She struggled, but, according to her perception, she did what she had to do.

You will hear me say this throughout the book: *people learn and operate at their own level of comprehension.* And what that means is, people live their lives and make decisions based on their mental capacity. Have you ever been drug induced or suffered from addiction? If not, it is important that you try not to judge what you do not understand. Most people would turn their nose up at a person addicted to drugs, and I probably would too, if it didn't hit close to home. However, my heart hurts for them. One bad decision or one small experiment can turn your world upside down.

I know in my heart that my mother would have been a great mother, if only she hadn't experimented with drugs—because she was before she developed the habit. I love my mother, but I do not like to see her in her condition, so I keep her at a distance. My defense mechanism: if you do not see it, it does not exist. Maybe it is my way of keeping the small memories I have of my mother before the drugs in my conscious mind. The things, such as my mother's drug addiction, that we push into or allow to fall deep into our unconscious mind allow us to run from them, to run from our reality. However, we can only run so far because they later show themselves in our actions and behaviors.

I have found that I have been craving that motherly affection and attention. I have unconsciously sought that love out from the mothers of those I have dated. As I reflect back, every relationship I have been in, my mates have always had really solid relationships with their mother. It was almost like an unwritten requirement for anyone I considered dating. In every relationship I have been in, it was always important for my mate's mother to like me and for me to build and foster that relationship with her. Every holiday and birthday, I made sure I reached out to them; I made sure I checked on them more than I did my own mother. I wasn't trying to replace my mother, but it hurt to yearn for a love from a woman unable to give it. I didn't want to resent my mother so I kept her at a distance, but I needed that motherly love. It makes a difference.

To all parents with daughters or caretakers of young girls—please hug her, and tell her she's beautiful.

Make sure she knows you love her.

Some people will spend so much time trying to be completely opposite of their mother or father, yet end up being just like them in a different capacity—for it is the parents who lay down the original foundation. A lack of love and affection is a feeling that money and material cannot replace; it too, is abandonment.

It is also important to note that when you are trying to be completely different from your mother, or your parent, you do not harm the child.

"We didn't have much growing up, so I am going to get my child whatever he/she wants."

Will that instill in them discipline, work ethic, respect and love? If you were to go today, would your child know how to function without you?

On the day you were conceived, was it love?

Reflect: What are you yearning?

What is something you did not receive as a child that you hope no one else goes without?

What are you giving to your child(ren) or the children you come into contact with? Is it love?

The Ugly Duckling

"Unconditionally love my beautiful ugly."
- Joe Budden

When is the last time you were called ugly and believed it? When you were younger, did the opposite sex flirt with you by picking on you? Did they call you ugly, or were you one of them? Do people now call you ugly? Do people flirt with you or keep you in the friend zone? How have you been taught to interact with the opposite sex based on your childhood experiences?

I remember my first boy crush. He was around my age and was a star basketball player, too. He was a cool dude, but I did not feel attractive enough for him. He was a star athlete and had a lot of girls crushing on him—but that did not stop me from admiring him from afar. Love is patient, right?

Wanting to be noticed, I made it my business to attend as many games as I could to make sure I cheered him on, thinking, "The more he sees me around, the more familiar he will become with me and, hopefully, he will begin to like me." WRONG!

He and I shared mutual friends. One day, one of our male friends decided to put us on a three-way phone call. My role was to be quiet and listen. (Although, looking back, I think this male friend set me up because he had a crush on me). As I sat quietly on the phone, my male friend says, "So what you think about Stephaine? She likes you." I knew it was coming, but accepting reality from someone you really like is tough.

Moments later I heard my crush say, "Man, she roasted." My heart felt like it broke into a hundred different pieces. I recall them laughing hysterically and having further conversation, which I do not remember as I tried to block everything out.

Oh, the beauty of growth…because I can laugh about it now—but, being a 7th grade girl, struggling with her identity and insecurities, that hurt more than a little. I had to trick myself into not liking him much after that. Why set yourself up for failure? Love isn't failure, is it? Or is love never giving up until you succeed after failure? I could not show I was hurt, but that one experience affected my mentality moving forward.

It was difficult for me to like someone after that because I really felt like the ugly duckling. It was not just that one situation, but that one situation was the icing on the cake. That one situation reassured me that maybe not hearing I was beautiful growing up was because I really wasn't beautiful.

From that day forward, I treated and approached all boys as if I was one of them, just as friends. Looking back, it is amazing how we allow someone's perception of us to change the perception we have of ourselves. In this case, instead of correcting the problem, I succumbed to it.

There I was, 13 years-old and heartbroken by someone I did not really know. I am not sure if his thoughts confirmed what I always thought about myself when I looked in the mirror, or if my need of wanting someone to love me grew from this experience to the point where I once again felt like a reject.

That experience set the tone for a lot of things moving forward in my life. I was afraid to express interest in others, I did not like taking pictures, I was afraid to look people in their eyes because I thought that everyone after him saw that same "roasted" girl. I resented my mother for sleeping with my father and creating me, maybe if she would have slept with someone better looking I would have turned out good enough—or maybe if my father would have slept with someone other than my mother.

Maybe if I would have had both parents around or even one, to build me up and tell me how beautiful I was, his perception of me would not have mattered as much and impacted me the way it did. Or maybe, if I did not exist life would be better for all; I thought that often growing up.

We all go through similar situations, some that seem very small, yet eventually have a bigger impact on us than we think. It is true that someone else's truth can hurt us if we have not owned our own truths. I ask myself now, when he expressed his truths about me to someone else, was it expressed with love? When I opened my ears to listen to his truth, was it done from love or was I hoping to fill a void?

*"Took something away out of every moment
I suffered, so y'all can go on and judge it."*
– Joe Budden

The ugly duckling lives to swim another day—there's hope.

I remember having my very first girl crush, after being turned down by a guy. Was it because I thought maybe girls would be easier? I remember the very first time I saw her. I had just finished practice at Riverside High School with my middle school team. The coach at Riverside asked me to stay and watch the game in hopes that I would consider attending school there in the fall.

I stayed with a few of my teammates, and I remember watching as the announcer announced her name, thinking, "Who is that?" I was intrigued by this stranger. The whole game, I paid attention to her every move. Not only was she a good basketball player, but I found myself physically attracted to her. This had never happened to me before. I was confused: girls are not supposed to like other girls, right? I cheered her on that night, but made a mental note to keep my distance; she was way out of my league, and I was not prepared to deal with another rejection.

Although in the moment I did not think about the situation with the previous young man I had a crush on, I still allowed an experience that hurt me to cripple me. I tried to push that experience to my unconscious mind, to not have to relive it; however, as I was getting ready to approach a similar situation—being vulnerable and liking someone, I ran. Instead of going after what I thought I wanted, I ignored my feelings and brushed them to the side. I could not confront them *with love*, so I left them alone. The insecurity and hurt that came from the previous situation unconsciously stopped me.

*"So if our paths happen to incidentally cross,
I pray that you can overlook all my miniature flaws."*
— Joe Budden

It was like our paths were bound to cross. All of a sudden, I would randomly see her at shoe stores, at basketball tournaments. In public of course, I didn't have the confidence to speak, so I just watched her from a distance. It was weird because, just a few weeks prior, I didn't even know she existed.

When I finally made it to high school, I was overly excited. I ended up selecting and attending Rufus King High School—not Riverside. I made the girls varsity basketball team my freshman year. Our team was on the rise, and things were looking good. Low and behold, my girl crush transferred schools and began playing for our rival school. (Talk about adrenaline and pressure!) I remember panicking about what hairstyle I would wear or how my uniform looked because I always wanted to appear presentable and "enough" in her eyes, and all I knew was her first and last name—funny how life works. It is amazing how people we do not know can have such a huge effect on us. We played basketball against each other quite a few times throughout my first two years in high school and gained a sense of respect for one another. We also shared the same space in more intimate settings a few times, due to mutual friends and playing for the same club team.

I remember the night we had our first memorable interaction. We were at our mutual friend's house—Keena (Rest peacefully)—and I was sitting on Keena's bed with other friends, my crush was laying there, and I was playing in her hair. I always hated my smile as a child, but I used to always hear people say (in general) you are more prettier when you smile so I tried to always smile while in her presence and laugh at small jokes that were being said to appear "prettier." Although I was smiling, I was scared shitless because I thought so highly of her. Everyone knew her, so many people liked her, men and women. However, there I was confused as to how I can like a girl, sad because I knew I wasn't secure in myself to ever be with someone like her, yet happy just to be soaking in the moment.

The next day at school, Keena walked up to me as I was sitting in the hallway (probably skipping class) and said, "Guess who said they were going to make you their wife?" I originally looked at her in disgust, honestly not knowing who she was going to say, but I knew it wasn't going to be my crush. Nonetheless, I asked, "Who?" As soon as she uttered the name of my crush, I instantly smiled from ear to ear wanting to know every detail. I was excited. I was happy. I was delighted. I was on cloud nine, but then reality kicked in...I am not pretty enough to be with someone like her, and that is just what it was. I look back now to the young girl I once was and back to this situation. Never once did Keena say, "Oh yeah, your crush said, 'One day you're going to be her wife, even though you are not pretty enough for her,'"—instead, from the beginning, I placed that limitation on myself, because, inside of me, love was not there from myself. Too often as people we put limitations on ourselves preventing us from experiencing and reaching our greatest potential. I was good enough to catch her interest and attention yet I lacked the substance because I did not love myself. Understand how powerful loving yourself really is.

Me not feeling pretty enough did not hinder our ability to be cordial, and it did not stop me from smiling when I was in her presence because that was the type of effect she had on me. She took time out to write me a letter. Was this an expression of love? Receiving this made me happy and made me feel special. Those are two emotions that should be associated *with love*, right? I wrote her a letter back because I wanted her to know that I indeed liked her, if not loved her. However, I knew at that time, I just was not ready. I was disappointed with myself for lacking the confidence. I was disappointed at her for being interested in me because that gave me hope. She moved on and got into a relationship. I found myself a little envious, but happy at the same time that she did not continue to pursue me because I would have ruined it. We remained friends and kept in contact with one another because that was the best thing for us at the time. There was actually a point in time when we told each other, "I love you" everyday. On most days, that was our only communication—"Hey, just saying I love you" and "I love you, too,"…nothing more and nothing less. But was it really love? What made it love? Or was it infatuation? Did we tell each other we loved each other because we really did, or was it the cool thing to do? Whatever the case is, that "I love you" allowed us to remain relevant in each other's lives, even if it was just as friends. The "I love you" allowed us to create our foundation, but did the fact that we did not fully understand what the "I love you" entailed taint our foundation unconsciously? Maybe the "I love you" was just like two friends saying, "I love you" to each other, but for me, it kept hope alive.

I do not think I ever let the thought of "us" go away. Was what I was experiencing love? Was I going to be missing out on my only opportunity to experience it because of my inability to love myself? It was tough watching her move on and be happy with someone else, but it was with love. Or was it?

And the duckling stays afloat

I remember having my first boyfriend; it was like it was yesterday. We shared the same first hour science class. He was a class clown that always kept me laughing and that laughter transpired into an old school puppy love. His ability to make me smile meant so much to me. It was in this moment I realized that looks aren't the only thing that matter. He and I bonded over jokes and never once did I stop and think, "Maybe he is laughing at me because he finds me unattractive." Coincidentally, being in chemistry class, chemistry was essential in making a connection with someone. This was a new experience for me. This had to be a prerequisite for love. I did not know this would be a lesson that would follow me throughout my life, but I knew that when I was smiling and happy—without forcing it— I felt good. I remember going around the school and telling people, "He is going to be my boyfriend one day."

I remember attending his basketball game at Marshall High School. He had just finished playing (he was on JV at the time), and we just so happened to be leaving the gym at the same time. He was with his dad, and I was with my friends. I'm not sure where I mustered up the courage, but I asked him, "So are you going to call me tonight?" His response, "I don't have your number." He then pulled out a dollar bill, I wrote my number down, and he called me that night.

That night, I did not allow my unconscious mind to distract me and hold me back. Was this love? Overcoming your fears and insecurities and going after what you want? It came so natural and the energy was mutual.

If only we could go back to those days when everything was so innocent. That night, we talked on the phone until 3:00 in the morning, even though we had school the next day. We laughed, we talked about each other, we got to know each other, and we had a really good age appropriate conversation (somehow conversations no longer happen that way). If only we could go back to the good old days. We also discovered we lived one house down from each other—this had to be fate!

We continued to become close, and eventually we became a couple on January 1st, 2003. It was almost just like the movie

Love & Basketball; he was my "Q." We even signed each other's basketball shoes. I remember losing my virginity to him on the couch at my cousin's house, where I resided, and forcing him to get our health book to ensure we were doing it properly. No one has ever had this conversation with me, and I knew I was not ready to become a mother, but I thought I was ready for him. Losing your virginity should be with someone special because that represents love, right?

Although I was happy to have a boyfriend that made me laugh, a boyfriend that helped me feel good about myself because I had someone to call my own, I was still dealing with my own issues, which ultimately contributed to our breakup. I didn't want him to talk to other girls too much or to play with them. I wanted to be his all and enough of everything, so he wouldn't want the attention of other girls—even at 15 years young.

In my mind, I finally had someone who told me he loved me regularly and who I loved doing things with, even if it was just riding to school with him and his mother each morning or catching the bus home from school. I found someone who I thought made me happy, and I didn't know how to keep it—so instead of cherishing it, unconsciously, I pushed it away. Here I was, a broken 16-year-old girl who was looking for a 16-year-old boy to fix me. How is that possible, when he can't even take care of or fix himself? This was my first heartbreak that I acknowledged at that point. If this is what love feels like, I didn't want it. Lost and confused, when we eventually broke up, my resentment toward my father and myself grew. How could I fail at happiness? Or was the happiness I was experiencing artificial and served as a temporary fill-in to help me later in life? Was everything I experienced *with love*? Or was it lust?

"Pop ain't called; he's still mad...
Still pissed, he's still angry.
I'm still going, no plan of slowing;
No way I'll ever let his immaturity taint me."
—Joe Budden

Often times, we aren't aware of the small situations and experiences that transpire to ultimately affect us. If a situation has caused us any sort of sadness or hurt we try to avoid dealing with it, so we push it to the back of our minds. We think that if we do not think about it, it does not exist; yet, we are wrong every time. The effects of those situations come out when we least expect them to, often disabling us. I was in a situation where I thought I was okay without my father. I was in a situation where I continued to add to my issues by bringing other people into my dysfunction and allowing them to dictate my worth based on what they were willing to give.

But the truth is, I still needed the love of my father because there I was looking for a 16-year-old to love me, to protect me, to save me everything I wished my father had done. Truth is, I had some things I needed to learn. The truth is also, I simply just did not love myself. True self-reflection, acceptance of one's truths, loving oneself, changed behavior and mental toughness helps grow that ugly duckling into a swan.

"I got a treasure, but it's content is invisible.
Was filled before with stuff that I thought I
treasured, but made me miserable.
My affairs together, here forever,
yeah, I'm back to work
Learned in order to lose love,
probably gotta have it first."
– Joe Budden

Reflect: Think about your first experience with liking someone, or think back to your first love.

Think about the emotions that were associated with those situations, and compare them to how you are in a relationship today.

Is what you are doing currently while in a relationship consistent to your first experience of a relationship? Or did your first experience of relationship change you?

Has it changed your mentality for the good or the bad? (Not including "ever since I have been single I have avoided headache" because you could be avoiding happiness, too).

Think about it, once we've been hurt, we try to avoid that feeling by any means necessary. As a result, we never really give people our true self, and without giving our true self how do you know you really are avoiding being hurt? The only person you end up hurting is yourself.

Do you want a family?

When you're sick, how important is it to have someone ease the pain?

When you've had a long day at work, how important is it for you to have someone to assist in taking the stress away—maybe with a nice massage, a warm embrace, or a home cooked meal?

When you have a brilliant idea, how important is it to have someone to share it with?

When you feel like a disappointment, how important is it to have that one person still rooting for you?

It is not about being able to call multiple people for different purposes; it is about having consistency with one. The energy you give and the energy you allow into your space is reflected in all of your day-to-day interactions, and everyone isn't deserving of your energy.

Take into consideration the men and women you interact with for different reasons...is it with love? Why or why not?

Define love.

What is it?

What do you want from it?

Relationships

"They say you are what you attract.
Here I am, screaming, 'Forget all of that'
Then I'm forced to believe
I attract and adore
a bunch of unstable broads
with character flaws"
– Joe Budden

In some sense, every relationship we have ever been in has been a reflection of our feelings as children. Although we grow up, the issues that we have never dealt with are still very immature. Every relationship we have been in is also a reflection of who we are today.

My high school sweetheart and I, although we only lasted a year, had a very up and down relationship throughout high school, as well as our early adult life. We were walking down two different paths but tried to stay connected, which was not the easiest. He was with someone, I was with someone, but we still had love for each other and, at the time, we still had the "one day we are getting married" kind of love. So what do you do when you have so much love for someone, but you are with someone else? NOTHING!

You watch from afar, you get mad when you see them doing stuff you wish they did with you, and you still hurt at the thought of the breakup even years later. Maybe that isn't the best thing to do, but that's what I did. This is the first guy who was open to loving me after I had been rejected, even though neither of us knew what love was.

This was the first guy that I allowed to get close to me. In my young mind, he was what I knew.

He and I had a bad falling out senior year, and later that year, he went to jail. What did I do? I received his letters and responded. Was this done out of love? Or was it my selfish need to want to keep him around? Or me wanting him to realize or feel guilty for leaving me and now needing me? Did he keep in contact with me because he was lonely? Or was it done out of love?

He was indeed my comfort zone. I believe and encourage people to step outside of their comfort zone because it pushes you in ways you would never think of. Stepping outside of your comfort zone allows freedom to grow, but what happens when you experience one loss after another or when life becomes too hard? You retreat back to your comfort zone; that is what happened between us.

Upon moving back to Wisconsin, we tried dating again, but at that point in his life, he had a flock of women around him that he entertained. The sad thing is, I was willing to settle until he was ready. Take what he was able to offer in hopes that it turned into something greater, but the truth is: how many other women are doing the same thing? Waiting around to be "chosen." I guess it's true, getting older does not automatically equate to maturity. I was willing to settle and play whatever role he wanted me to in order to feel loved, but is that really love? I thought so. He never completely cut me off, so that had to mean there was some love there right? This seemed to be a pattern for me. Older in age, but immature in mind because I did not see my own worth.

As women, this happens often. We are afraid to venture off and start new because we never know what we are going to get. Instead, we stick to what we know because at least we know what we are dealing with and what to expect, even if it is far less than we deserve. Now the question comes, is it love? Not that you have for him or her, but to stay in that situation, is it love for self?

Thank God I soon grew impatient. Tired of waiting. Tired of feeling like I wasn't good enough for him to make me his girlfriend. Tired of the inconsistency. Even in our young adulthood, we found ourselves going through similar situations we did as

teens. I was usually sad, upset and acting out.
Is this really love? Or were we trying to hold
on to a memory? Just like that, one month
after I chose to walk away, I found myself in
a relationship. It could not have been love.

*"When you stubborn and prideful
not much is insightful,
but God was trying to show me
something.
He ain't think that I knew
sometimes shit that doesn't breathe
can die, too."*
–Joe Budden

Sometimes we keep people around for our own selfish reasons. Some reasons are very obvious and others are a secret to us and those around us. It is not until we are real with ourselves that it becomes clear.

I knew that I loved him and that he loved me, but were we supposed to love each other romantically? More in-depth? More intimately? I learned that just because you love a person, does not mean you are supposed to be in a relationship with them.

So maybe because we experienced a lot together, maybe it was love—just not the kind of love two people have for one another that makes the other better. It was not the kind of love where you get butterflies in your stomach, and you are just happy to be with that person where there are no restrictions.

Loving someone does not always mean you two will live happily-ever-after; it just simply means: you love them. There are a few different ways you can love a person, and one of those ways is by just being friends with them.

Once he and I stripped our title away and stopped trying to be together intimately, the dynamics of our relationship changed, and we were able to take it for what it was worth things gradually became better. We are able to enjoy each other's company without drama, our chemistry is more organic, and we are able to laugh with one another, talk in-depth about our personal problems without feeling judged, hold each other accountable and be real with each other. We are able to hang out and not care what other people think—because, now, we are able to embrace the true purpose of being in each other's lives, so we are able to be friends with love.

Reflect: Who or what are you holding onto that you need to let go of, so you can move on?

The Saga Continues

Remember the girl crush I had in 8th grade? Well, that crush-turned-love traveled with me all the way into adulthood.

I moved away for 6 years to attend school, and she and I remained in contact with one another. When I moved back home, we began to spend a lot of time together. Eventually, that led to us, finally, becoming a couple. That relationship lasted three whole years, with us never once breaking up.

When you love someone, even if it is just the thought, you are never prepared for it to end, even if the signs are there.

When you want something for so long and you finally get it, it's exciting. It almost feels like an accomplishment, and I had to ask myself was it pride? Or was it love? Did the desire of fulfilling this accomplishment of being with this specific person after wanting her for so long cloud my judgement? Or was this really my opportunity to finally feel what love is?

I honestly thought this was it. In the moment I was asked to be her girlfriend I was ecstatic. Although still very nervous, it seemed like the perfect set-up.

*"I mean, we started with love;
the beginning was magical."*
—Joe Budden

14 Days of Love

After spending a lot of time together, both intimately and among friends, I felt it was time to make a move. For me, love was going after what you want.

It started on February 1st through February 14th, and each day I did something different and special to demonstrate my love for her because love is expressive actions. With the help of a couple of friends, it turned out perfectly! On the 14th day, she asked me to be her girlfriend. This woman who 7 years prior, said she was going to make me her wife asked me to be her girlfriend. Based on what I mentioned before about the love I had for her and the way we were in each other's lives, one would assume this was a match made in heaven. At least I did. It was fate that brought us back together, It was our love for one another that was going to make this work, right?

Let's rewind for a second. I had been single for a year and a half, after a three-year relationship that did not end ideally. I did not take much time to recover and examine myself because, in between that time, I spent a huge bulk of time trying to work it out with my ex.

She was in a situation herself, prior to us becoming one; so, we both came with baggage.

Now, as a career woman, how do you be a girlfriend? I was not the same woman I had been a year prior. I had more responsibilities and more goals. As a woman unsure of herself, how do you give of yourself? At the same time, how often does a shot at love, that you feel genuine about, come around? I had to make a decision.

When I said yes, I said yes because of my feelings and love for her, but when I said yes, I think I cheated us both out of a true depiction of what love could be and stripped us of reaching our greatest potential of loving each other because I was not ready.

I simply was not ready. I was not ready to be with her. Her presence still intimidated me. The thought of other women liking her still bothered me. No, I was not ready. Instead of being honest with her, and instead of being honest with myself, I pretended I was ready (because I did love her). I genuinely thought we could make it work, and that we would have a whole love story that we can write about once we get it right.

I had a plan, and my motto was simple: make sure she has everything she wants and needs, so that she remains happy enough to be oblivious to my flaws while I secretly work on them. I know I am not the only one who has been in a situation in which we tried to cover our insecurities by over compensating in material things, time and attention.

That seemed to have worked for the first year of our relationship. It was when we started to experience difficulties and disagreements that our truth was exposed: we weren't meant to be together; the timing was simply off. I entered the relationship with a plan, but love is unconditional right? Yet, there I was, subconsciously, putting conditions on our love.

She entered the relationship with her own scars, but with her guards down, open to loving and being loved in return. It was the hidden agenda that separated us. A hidden agenda that I did not fully know existed, but a hidden agenda that stemmed from my own insecurities. I spent a lot of time trying to sweep under the rug, hoping that receiving enough love would eventually overshadow any ill feelings I may have had of myself. Though there were ill feelings, I was not going to admit to it. There were times she would call me out about being "insecure" and it would upset me. I am not sure what upset me more, the fact that it was true or the fact that she could not help me. Every time that she brought it up, I denied it.

A relationship is more than just two people coming together and spending time together. In order to make a relationship between two people work, both parties have to be open and honest about who they are and what they want. We never had a plan, we were just together.

How many of you are currently in a relationship without a plan? Without a plan you fail to move forward. You will continue to find yourself wasting time.

When two people come together, rarely is one person a complete package. When we begin to date, we have this long laundry list of qualities and traits that we want from another person (often these traits come from ones we observed, likely from our caretakers). Once we find someone we think is worth being in a relationship with, we then expect for them to be perfect for us. Yet, we are not perfect for them. So, instead of taking time out to learn the other individual and how you two work and grow together, we grow apart. Instead of treating a relationship like a partnership, we grow individually which recreates little overlap. Now we are stuck being a boyfriend/girlfriend to someone we do not know; someone we do not want to be with.

Knowing your mate is so critical. I know I was not the easiest to love, but while in our relationship, I asked for three things. Three things that did not make or break our relationship, but three things that mattered to me: random "I love yous," random compliments, and kisses on the forehead. I do not know if me asking her for these three things were retaliation for her calling me insecure, because now when she called me insecure my rebuttal could be, "but you can't even compliment me, of course, I am insecure." Maybe it was my safety net. It would not have cured the problem, but it could have helped. It is possible I was in denial, and as much as I wanted her to be oblivious to my flaws, I was crying out for help. I still wanted her to love me, and I needed her to break down my walls.

Lesson: Often times, we have our walls up waiting for someone to tear them down, yet not allowing them to. It is like watching someone try to use a wrench to nail down a picture when you know all they need is a hammer. The lack of communication is what is killing relationships today. No one wants to be honest out of fear of looking weak, in the eyes of the one they love. If they see you as weak then they will stop loving you because love is strong, right? So we hide from the truth and expect them to love the false us, but they can't. How can you want someone to help you when you're lying about needing help?

"More angles, a million different looks
Was on the same page,
just in different books
there's so much I want to say,
but I got no ground
because we ain't break up,
more like broke down."
–Joe Budden

We were two individuals who were tainted from wasting time in previous relationships who were really optimistic about making this one work due to our love for one another, but optimism without effort can only get you so far.

It was ideal. We had known each other for quite some time; we shared some of the same interests; we felt with two different personalities, we could learn from each other; we knew each other's friends and family; it felt destined to be. Again, just because you love a person, does not mean you have to be with that person.

Keep in mind, we were friends for a long while before becoming a couple, and when we finally became a couple we realized how much about each other we did not know. As a result, from the beginning, our foundation was tainted.

Friendship is a great foundation for a relationship, but what kind of friends are you?

The kind that speak when you see each other and there's no real substance, but you've never had a problem with one another, so you're friends?

The kind that share intimate secrets with one another?

The kind that knows what the other is thinking?

The kind made from convenience?

The kind where you use the "friendship" title to cover up how you really feel?

Re-evaluate the foundation of your relationship. What is it really built on?

How well do you really know your partner? That is what's important.

The thought of finally finding someone who is open to love you, the thought of building on a friendship, the thought of being with someone who makes your day better and who supports your dreams and aspirations all sounds great—only to find out we spent three years in a relationship and barely knew each other.

I mean, we knew the basics and can share with you things about each other that many probably will not know, but the transparency, the growth, and the togetherness, all of that was missing.

I spent so much time running from myself and covering my tracks that I did not have time to get to know her on the level that you are supposed to know your mate on. We were so different, but I believed that opposites attract. I learned that opposites do attract but only when there's a mutual goal in mind. Opposites attract when one can learn from the other person what they are missing within themselves. The true reality was simple: we weren't made to love each other in the capacity which we tried to in that moment of our lives. However, we did try.

"How could you make something so ugly out of what was once beautiful."
– Joe Budden

The relationship lacked substance. There was little growth on either parts because we spent so much time being upset and arguing with each other over things that were so small. This prevented us from growing as people because when a person has such an impact on your life, the energy coming from that relationship follows you throughout your day-to-day activities.

We became so comfortable with the insanity that we never really dealt with the issues. It goes back to what I said in the beginning of the book, *How you learned what love is, often times, is completely different from how the person you are interested in learned what love is. Meanwhile, we all become fixated in operating in our own space.* We were both tainted, and our ideas of love were different. We did not care to peel back the layers and learn how to love each other the way we each needed to be loved.

For us, it looked good on paper, and we did love each other to an extent, but because we tried to hold onto something that was not meant to be at the time, we ruined a friendship.

"Got memories,
but at what point are they lost?
You say we could work through it,
at what point is it forced?
We should have never rushed."
– Joe Budden

I remember not wanting my partner to get too close to anyone other than me. I used to first say it was because you never know people's intentions—which is still partially true—but since then, I have learned it was because I didn't want to be exposed.

As I was silently dealing with my own battles, I did not want my mate to see that confidence in someone else that they did not see in me.

We have all been there before. Checking our mates' social media pages, disliking other men and women who may be interested in our mate because we do not want to be exposed. Most of us have fallen victim to the societal trend that we have to be "crazy," "jealous," or "an undercover detective" in order to show our mates that we love them; that is not love. Those are signs of us acting out due to experiences we have pushed into our unconscious mind. If you find yourself being either, maybe you should take a break from dating. Associating yourself with any of the aforementioned qualities only perpetuates a cycle of hurt and anger and further pushes us away from the truth.

The true reality is, you cannot stop a person from doing what he/she wants to do. No matter how crazy or how much of a detective you are. That person cannot love you into not being crazy, jealous or an undercover detective: that is a reflection of you.

The more I acted out, the more I showed my hand, the more obvious it was that it just was not the right time.

We should have been more patient. We should have taken the time to figure each other out and to figure out ourselves and how and where we fit into the equation.

Too often we find ourselves living a lie.

We live a life that is not ours to be more appealing to others.

Those relationships will fail every time.

"What hurts more?
The act of getting cut off
or realizing that your two cents wasn't
worth more."
– Joe Budden

The end was bittersweet, literally. I was hurt when she left. The whole time I was preparing to settle, she was plotting her getaway, unbeknownst to me. I begged and pleaded with her to stay. I tried to communicate every reason she should stay, and it all fell on numb ears.

At this point it was too late, yet it was right on time. I am not sure what it was that hurt me most:

1. The realization that our comfort had come to an end, and I would be forced to think outside of the box.
2. The feeling of betrayal because I thought we were living in this insanity together.
3. Her ability to shut me out and not feel remorseful.
4. The fact that I had contributed to yet another failed relationship.
5. The fact that I was losing, what I thought was, the love of my life.

Although I went into that relationship guarded, I lost myself in an attempt to become everything I thought my mate wanted. Not only was I my own walking unconscious thoughts and feelings, but I added more baggage. When you hide behind so many faces to cover your own, how do you know which one to wear when you are all out of faces? Often times it is not the perception other people have of us, it is our belief of what other people's perception of us is, which stems from our belief of ourselves. At some point we have to realize that we are enough.

I lost myself by trying to hide myself. Never lose yourself.

"So,

the break up never really was a plan to me.
In retrospect,
I think I was complacent with insanity.
We were so exhausted, bored with—tortured
But since I couldn't picture my life without
you, I fought it."
– Joe Budden

I did not know how I would move forward. I was not sure I could move forward. I tried to fight for us. The more I did, the more I pushed her away and the more I sunk into depression.

The only two people I felt I could love genuinely, in that capacity, no longer served that role. I wanted to hate her, to resent her, for her to hurt like I did, but I also wanted to love her, to nurture her because I know I had damaged her.

The way in which my relationships ended became a pattern. I questioned myself and my self-worth. I spent many days and nights alone, without turning on any lights and barely eating. It was in these moments I realized, the only person I should be upset with is myself. The one person I have the potential to create, love and nurture—the most important person needing me—was myself.

It was not how I would have liked it to go and probably worse than any breakup I have experienced, but it forced me to own my truths, which has helped me grow in ways I could not have ever fathomed. I had every intention to love her. I wanted to love her like no one has ever loved her and like no one has ever loved me. I was determined of this, but I failed because I did not know how to, like many of us. We think we do, but we all have issues we need to confront.

She believed in me, let her guards down, and I let her down. To this day, truthfully, it hurts to think about it because she trusted me; however, "there is beauty in every ugly." Everything we went through, we were supposed to go through, so I would not change anything. Likewise, everything you are going through, you are supposed to be going through.

There comes a time when you have to be real, stop placing the blame, and take ownership in who you are. I do not fully think everything we went through was completely my fault, but I can't shame someone who took such a monumental journey with me and taught me so much about myself. I can only own my truth. I have lots of questions, but I had to ask myself, "Would the answer bring me love?"

We both deserve someone better fit for us.

I learned a very valuable lesson throughout this process: be true to who you are, and those who are supposed to love you, will. I will always love you.

"So love isn't lost,
I know exactly where I put it at."
– Joe Budden

So often we seek things from others that we never provide information about. We become one with people and expect them to know what we need with no blueprint, no love book for dummies, and no instructions. We expect them to just figure it out—no guide, no map, no outlined routes.

Then we take our frustrations out on them when they don't get it right. The thing is, people react and respond based on their own level of understanding when they lack our input and insight. As people, we do not know what we do not know, and without the proper guidance and knowledge we will never know.

"Momma said,
'Why can't you ever be alone?'"
– Joe Budden

I've spent time in relationships that I didn't see a future in, but the idea is having someone so that you're never alone, right? WRONG!

When you approach relationships that way, when there is a hidden agenda or when one partner is more invested than the other, someone gets hurt. In the midst of me trying to find love, the one love I needed, I was running from: love from myself.

No one can heal you, and no one can love you when you do not love yourself. When you are lost, no one can find you—not even you. You become someone you said you would never be, and everything you shoved to your unconscious mind, you are now confronted with—just in a new environment, with new players, at a new time.

If you have not noticed, I chose to only speak about two of my five relationships because these two illustrated the cycle I was stuck in the cycle that kept me in a comfort zone. A cycle that made me feel safe because I could tolerate what I was given. The cycle that did not promote my growth, instead, enabled my dependency on others to make me feel secure within myself.

Once that cycle was finally broken, as a young adult, there I was finally facing every issue I had run from: the fear of being rejected, not feeling wanted, suffering from low self-esteem, experiencing inconsistencies, and not having or experiencing true love from a parent.

Due to these things, I was willing to settle and force relationships with individuals because, at one time, they showed me love and were willing to fill a void, and I was willing to accept whatever they were offering in order to feel complete. What I didn't know then, was that I was the only one who could complete that puzzle.

No matter how much they loved me, no matter how much they showed me, I was blocking love the whole time. I blocked love with fear, insecurity, anxiety and selfishness. Was it really love? A part of me still feels as though I owe them the whole me because they did try with love. Then the other part of me feels as though I do not owe them much more and that we were all a part of a big lesson, and that is reward enough.

"I more than owe my life to you, I'm forever in debt."
– Joe Budden

Neither of us had the capacity to love wholly, at those times. I have learned to release, forgive others and myself, to forgive my parents and to deal with any issue head on-starting with all experiences that were tainted by better judgement since I can remember.

I found myself in relationships with good people who were wrong for me, and I tried to love them selfishly, conditionally, when it was convenient. I wanted it to be easy. I was loving at my level of comprehension.

My love was just a product of that of my mother and father; the apple does not fall too far from the tree.

Reflect: Thoroughly evaluate your current relationship:

Is it love, or is there a hidden agenda?

Have you grown while in your relationship? How? Why or why not?

If that person never said, "I love you," would you know they loved you? How would you know?

Are you running from anything? If so, what?

Stages

Anger

Anger is an emotion characterized by antagonism toward someone or something you feel has deliberately done you wrong. Who are you angry at?

For so long, I was angry, and I never knew it. Instead, I covered it up as if nothing was wrong. What I was going through was normal, I mean it was all I knew. Being angry is a natural emotion: things happen, you get upset, then life goes on. However, what happens to the angry emotion you've never dealt with? The anger that every trigger continues to add weight to what is already there? You become angrier, and then you explode.

I remember having the worst reputation for being mean and fighting because I didn't trust people. The inconsistency in my life, early on, proved to me that people get what they want from you and then let you go. I remember fighting in the alley for chump change just so my younger sister and I could buy something to eat from the gas station. I remember losing a fight and crying as I continued to talk so much smack. Was that love? Was I put in those situations to prepare me for the many fights life was going to throw my way?

I was angry when I never had a parent attend my basketball games or school performances. I was angry when my father did finally show up to my 8th grade graduation. I intentionally did not smile in any of the pictures I took with him. I was angry when I had to wear a blue jean Pocahontas sleeveless shirt with a blue jean Nike tennis skirt to school on the first day because that's all we could afford. I was angry when I thought others were treated better than me because they looked better than me.

I was angry because there was no consistency in my life. I watched people come and go, and it made me question if I was good enough or not.

"I used to always try to be good enough,
and couldn't figure out why
I wasn't good enough,
so instead of being good enough
I just want to be better than good enough."
– Joe Budden

At basketball games, I remember being ejected and kicked out of leagues, because I was angry. People knew me as the young girl with the bad attitude. So many people wrote me off without trying to understand who I was and why I acted out in the ways I did…and that made me angry.

It's like they put me in a box and didn't care about me. In relationships, I was angry. I was angry when they just didn't get "it." I was angry when they called me out on my internal battles I was facing (insecurity and jealousy) because I felt exposed. I was exposed, yet I was not receiving help. It felt like I was drowning.

To cover up the anger I had inside of me, I tried to show love and care for those around me. I tried creating the environment I yearned for; however, I couldn't stay consistent due to my own battles. I tried to fill a void by overly caring for others, but that wasn't love.

Often times, we do things because we think we are supposed to, and we are not necessarily genuine in the process. When you find yourself doing things for the wrong reasons you will never attain the sense of fulfillment you seek.

Reflect: How do you show anger?

What is something that angers you now, and why? Does it have a hold on you?

How was anger expressed or suppressed among the people around you?

What is your earliest memory of being angry? With whom were you angry, and how did you handle this situation?

What is something you would like to accomplish by releasing your anger?

Acceptance

We never like to hear people tell us about ourselves, especially when what they are saying isn't the most pleasant. In the eyes of others, we want to be seen in a certain light, but how can you be seen in a light that you do not belong in?

There comes a time when we have to own our truths. However, it is not the easiest because we run from things we are ashamed of. Nonetheless, one of life's greatest beauties is the ability to change. Change is inevitable. Change can be for the good or for the bad, depending on how you choose to look at it.

Most people resist change because the unknown is scary. People would rather stick to what they already know because they know what they are going to get. However, remaining in your comfort zone only allows you to stay where you are. Learn who you are, accept who you are and own who you are. You are the only person who can hold you back.

Reflect: What are you currently holding onto that is comfortable? Something that is affecting you negatively or positively?

Challenge yourself, why is it comfortable? How can you get better?

What is something you currently have not accepted about yourself that would be beneficial to accept?

Utilize your support system.

We live in a world of 8 billion people, some good, others lessons. It is not meant for you to go through life alone. We, as people, have a tendency of running from one person to the next, in an attempt to protect our weaknesses and flaws.

When we are going through things, the last thing we want to do is let someone know we are going through things. This comes out of fear of being judged or being seen as weak, especially when we are perceived as strong.

For so long, I dealt with my issues alone. For so long, I walked around trying to keep my head held high while trying to maintain a smile. For so long, I didn't trust to bear my soul to the people around me. For so long, I was surrounded by so many people, yet I was still very much alone.

It is so important to utilize the people in your life in a productive way. Some people were put in our lives for very specific purposes. Once we come to terms that we aren't experts in everything, the easier our lives become.

Reflect: Make a list of the most important people in your life.

What are their roles?

What can you depend on them for?

What capacity should you avoid depending on them for?

Forgiveness

Most people think forgiveness is having to put yourself in the same situation because someone said, "I am sorry," and you accepted their apology. However, forgiveness is more of an inner peace.

Forgiveness is knowing you have learned from any given situation that may have caused you hurt, anger or sadness and applying those emotions in a productive way. Forgiveness is not about forgetting. It is about being able to think about those moments and feel a sense of relief while thinking, "I made it through that."

Forgiveness does not come overnight. It takes time, and sometimes you are not aware that you need to forgive. Often times, forgiveness is not led by, "I am sorry" from the perpetrator. At some point you have to realize forgiveness is about you.

Give yourself time. The scars took time to form, so, understand, learning to forgive takes times to heal. Forgiveness is the start of the healing process, but when you decide you are ready and able to forgive, make sure it is with love.

For so many of my adolescent years, I was angry. Angry at not being able to do "mother-daughter" things, angry I couldn't engage in conversations about parents, angry I had to work more than other kids my age to be able to provide myself with basic necessities—because of that, I had to grow up sooner, and I was angry I couldn't be a child longer. I was angry because people did not think I was pretty, angry because at 14, I had stresses and worries. I was angry because I couldn't experience trips to get my nails and hair done or get new clothes often. I was angry that people categorized me as an "at-risk" youth, angry that people labeled me as having a bad attitude. I was angry that most people wrote me off and never took the time to get to know me.

What we see on the surface is never a true a depiction of a person, just the aftermath. Stuck in our own truths and weighed down by our own realities, we never take too much time getting to know a person. Instead, we see what we see, we try to fix them and then, we shut down and run away when they refuse our help.

As people, we are not experiments. We have feelings, emotions, pains and sorrows that we haven't learned to deal with, and society has taught us to hide them.

When something goes wrong, do you think to yourself, "Why? Why me?" I did, and I'm pretty sure that we all do. The feeling of loneliness made me feel as though I was better off not here. Why must things happen to innocent people? What did I do? I didn't ask to be born.

All questions I used to ask, but then one day a bulb went off:

Despite how your life started off, you can create your happy ending—but you have to work on it, and that does include dealing with issues head-on, forgiving those who hurt you and graciously walking away from things that hinder your success, discourage your progress and/or strips you of your energy.

Reflect: Who do you need to forgive?

Why haven't you forgiven them yet? What is holding you back?

What are you still holding onto and what about that situation is preventing you from moving forward?

Dealing with you

Please note, we can only be experts of our own lives because we are stuck with our own truths, experiences and skeletons. We are the only ones who know what can break us or make us. We are the only ones who have a better idea as to why we tend to do the things we do and why we run from our need to do other things.

Everything I make mention to is all my own perspective. One of our biggest issues is that we spend so much time trying to diagnose each other. We spend so much time pointing the finger at others. We spend so much time justifying our own actions by making it about someone else.

If you ask anyone why they are the way they are, most people will begin with a list of people that contributed to why they are how they are. In a lot of cases, we really are the reason why some people are the way they are. The time we cheated on them, lied to them, stole from them, used them, babied them, walked out on them—so you have to ask yourself, where is this energy coming from? Is it love, or is it fear? Is it selfishness, and, if so, why are you acting out of selfishness?

We take a piece of every person we encounter and share space with, and, in return, we leave a little piece of us with them. When you leave a piece of you behind, is it love? Most times, we leave behind negative energy with people we thought we loved because we are not doing it out of love. However, why are we doing it?

Finding time for self after a bad experience—most people skip that process, so they never truly heal. Get to know yourself, and let the past be the past. There is a reason things happen the way they do. We only get caught in the revolving door of the bad karma when we continue to allow ourselves to get stuck.

"Sad part is,
you never have the same dream twice."
– Joe Budden

Identity

Who are you?

What do you stand for?

When you leave this earth, what will you leave?

What will you be known for? How proud of you will your children be that you are their parent?

In life, we're tugged this way and that way, and we go on roller coaster rides—up and down, around and around. Every situation we've ever been in, every person we've ever encountered, we take a little piece of them with us.

When we are constantly surrounded by people, always involved in things, we subconsciously begin to pick up and develop habits. That is because, as people, we tend to adapt to our environment. When you are unsure of yourself, it is easy to get lost and become someone you do not know.

After any situation, it is imperative to take the time to weed out the lessons you learn and apply them to your life as you move forward. The amount of time you take to re-define and re-learn yourself is all dependent on you, and it is critical to your progression.

It is important not to base your progression on the next person's progression. Spend some time alone, learn your strengths, and expand on them. Learn your weaknesses, and work on them. Life is not a race so take your time creating the most beautiful journey you can.

Next time someone asks you who you are, be able to answer them without hesitation. Be confident in your role in the world, and continue to build on it.

Don't get stuck. There is a lesson in everything that happens—one that is molding you.

Look in the mirror, and answer the question:

WHO ARE YOU?

"I broke down a while ago,
finally picking up the pieces,
memoirs of how
the undefeated can feel depleted."
– Joe Budden

Lessons Learned:

There's been a point in all of our lives in which we all felt insecure about something. Some of us can admit it, while some of us need to admit it, and yet others of us will probably never admit it. The lesson comes into play when you are honest with yourself. For so long, I did not want to look in a mirror; for so long, I did not want to take a picture; for so long, when I did see a reflection of me, I would cringe. I learned to not like my outward appearance because of what others thought about it, and that pain alone made me run from myself.

Up until my 28th birthday party, I allowed the well-being of others to replace the well-being of myself—thinking, "If they are busy being happy, they wouldn't be able to see how unhappy I truly was." I had run from myself for so long, that I was not aware of my full potential.

I know, "Self-love is the best love" is a bit cliché; however, it is true. If I never decided to be so open or never decided to write this book no one would have had any idea how I truly felt about myself at critical moments in my life. Moments that were designed to either make me or break me.

The only reason they did not break me is because I chose, with time, to take the lesson out of everything and every situation I have been in and, through self-reflection, decided to pursue my desire to grow.

It all comes full circle. How we are taught to love, to show love, to receive love and what love is, is based on what love was for us as children. Nowadays, parents are having children and are forced to parent children while still subconsciously dealing with issues they developed when they were children, which they thought they buried.

Parents: deal with your own issues as you prepare to care for a child because your issues become their issues. Talk with your children, do things with your children, pave the foundation that you want your children to build from, and encourage them along the way. If you have no clue on how to begin or you find yourself in a pattern of unhealthy relationships—keep in mind, if it is unhealthy for you, it is unhealthy for your children, too—simply, start with you.

On the day your child was conceived,
was it love?

When your next child is conceived,
will it be love?

On the night you were conceived,
was it love?